**THE BRITISH
HORSE SOCIETY**

C000214255

SOMERSET ON HORSEBACK

AVAILABLE IN THIS SERIES

The Cotswolds on Horseback
Wiltshire on Horseback
Westmorland on Horseback
The Ridgeway Downs on Horseback
Exmoor on Horseback
Somerset on Horseback
Hampshire on Horseback
Leicestershire & Rutland on Horseback

First published 1994
by The British Horse Society
Access & Rights of Way Department
British Equestrian Centre
Stoneleigh Park, Kenilworth
Warwickshire CV8 2LR

A catalogue record for this book is available from the British Library

ISBN 1 899016 05 8

Printed by:
Tripod Press Limited, 7 Wise Street, Leamington Spa, CV31 3AP

Distribution: The British Horse Society, Stoneleigh Park, Kenilworth,
Warwickshire, CV8 2LR

CONTENTS

TRAILS

ACKNOWLEDGEMENTS

A number of people and organisations have given their time and expertise to provide details for this book and open up the trails.

In particular, the British Horse Society would like to thank Vanda Coulsey, Peter Marzetti, Tina Mortimer, Belinda Burne, Diana Pearce, Georgina Hoskyns, Venetia Craggs, Anthony John, Pam Gormley and Stephanie Wheeler, for surveying, developing and describing the routes. Julia Dawn for her commendable fund raising efforts. Noel & Helen Edmonds and Bob Langrish (photographer) for the cover picture. All members of the South Somerset District Council Management Section, the Somerset County Council Rights of Way Group and the Quantock Hills Warden Service for their advice, guidance and assistance in opening and waymarking routes; but above all to Somerset County Council and South Somerset District Council for such generous financial support.

FOREWORD

The '................. on Horseback' series of published rides launched in 1993 has proved extremely popular. This confirms the British Horse Society's belief that many riders need information on routes known to be open, available and providing pleasurable riding.

Many volunteers have worked to research these routes, thus helping to contribute to the Countryside Commission's target of having all rights of way defined, open and signed by the year 2000. This Society wholeheartedly supports this aim which it incorporates into its Access & Rights of Way strategy for the last decade of this Century.

Together with our booklet 'Bed & Breakfast for Horses', these publications enable riders and carriage drivers to plan holidays and other trips. This extends the pleasure and value of owning a horse either to ride or drive, and enables an assortment of different experiences to be enjoyed be they landscape, flora and fauna or historic sites and buildings.

Equestrianism provides one of the most intense pleasures of life, wholly understood only by those who ride or drive carriages. The Society is proud to contribute in some way to the fulfilment of that pleasure. The challenges of research and development of further routes will continue to be explored.

E A T BONNOR-MAURICE
Chairman, British Horse Society

March 1994

INTRODUCTION

The British Horse Society's ARROW Project aims to identify open and usable routes of varying length and shape (circular, figure-of-eight or linear) to help riders and carriage drivers to enjoy the countryside by means, as far as possible, of the network of public rights of way and the minor vehicular highways. This collection of rides is the result of research and mapping by volunteers who took up the challenge of the ARROW initiative with such enthusiasm and effort.

I am faced with the equally daunting challenge of writing an introductory chapter. Should I write reams about each topic or try simply to point you in the right direction? I have decided upon the second method as the search for information is itself highly educative and stays in the mind better than reading it all in one place. Also, since we all have different expectations of our holiday, a very full guide seemed wrong. Nevertheless, there are a few pointers I would like to suggest to you.

The most important one is to start your planning several months in advance of the trip, including a visit to the area you intend to ride in. You should make endless lists of things to DO (e.g. get the saddle checked) and things to CHECK OUT (can you read a map, for instance). You may find joining the local BHS Endurance Riding Group very helpful, as there you will meet people who can give you information about the degree of fitness needed for yourself and your horse (feeding for fitness not dottiness) , and many other useful hints on adventurous riding. You may also enjoy some of the Pleasure rides organised by the group or by the local Riding Club. These are usually about 15-20 miles and you ride in company,

though using a map. You may find them under the title Training Rides. These rides will get both of you used to going into strange country. If you usually ride on well-known tracks, then your horse will find it nerve-racking to go off into new territory, and you yourself may also find the excitement of deep country a bit surprising, so try to widen your experience at home before you go off on holiday.

ACCOMMODATION

Decide how far you wish to ride each day of your holiday, book overnight accommodation for both of you and if possible visit it to see if the five-star suite on offer to your horse is what he is used to. Decide if you want to stable him or to turn him out at the end of the day, and arrange to drop off some food for him, as he will not relish hard work on a diet of green grass, nor will he enjoy a change in his usual food. If you are to have a back-up vehicle, of course, then you will not need to do some of this, but you should certainly make a preliminary visit if you can. The BHS publish a Bed & Breakfast Guide for Horses which is a list of people willing to accommodate horses, and sometimes riders, overnight. The Society does not inspect these places, so you should check everything in advance.

FITNESS

You and your horse should be fit. For both of you , this is a process taking about two months. If you and/or your horse are not in the full flush of youth, then it may take a bit longer. The office chair, the factory floor, or the household duties do not make or keep you fit, but carefully planned exercise will. Remember that no matter how fit your horse seems, he does not keep himself fit - you get him fit. There are several books with details of fitness programmes for a series of rides. Do not forget to build in a rest day during your holiday - neither of you can keep going all the time, day after day. Miles of walking may get you fit, but it uses different muscles from riding; you may get a surprise when you start riding longer distances. It seems to me that the further you intend to ride, the longer your preparation should be. Nothing can be done in a hurry.

Your horse should be obedient, so work on that. If you want him to stand, then he must stand. If you want to go through water, then he must be prepared to walk down a slope or even step down off a bank to go through the stream, so start with puddles and insist that he go through the middle. Does he help you open gates? I hope so, or you will have a great deal of mounting and dismounting to do. Does he tie up - this is essential if you are to have a peaceful pint at lunchtime.

MAPS

Can you read a map? Can you make and read a grid reference (usually referred to as GR)? Get a Pathfinder map of your area and take yourself for a walk and see if you end up where you expect to. Learn to know exactly where you are on the map, and how to understand the symbols (if your map shows hilly ground, the journey will take longer). Can you work out how long a ride is in miles and roughly how long it will take? You will be using rights of way and it is very important that you stay in the line of the path - that is the only place you have a right to be, and you may deviate from that line only as much as is necessary to get you round an obstruction on the path. You are going to be riding over land that forms part of someone's work place

and that fact must be respected. It is only by the efforts of farmers and landowners that the countryside exists in its present form - so that we may enjoy it as we pass by.

You will need to know the grid reference (GR.) of the start and end of the various tracks you are to use. Get a copy of an Ordnance Survey (OS) Landranger map and really learn the details on the right-hand side, some of which explain how to arrive at a Grid Reference. Learn to go in the door (Eastings - from left to right) and up the stairs (Northings - from bottom to top). There is a great deal of information on the Landranger maps and not so much on the Pathfinders, but the Pathfinder gives more details on the map itself, so that is the map you will use for the actual ride. Or you may care to buy a Landranger of the area you are visiting and, using a highlighter pen, mark in all the rides you want to make, so that you can see through the marks you make. Then get from any Outdoor shop a map case which will allow you to read the map without taking it out of the case and which you can secure round yourself. Also, you should know if you are facing north, south, east or west as you ride. Quite important if you think about it, as it is no good riding into the sunset if you are meant to be going south. Plastic orienteering compasses are cheap and reliable.

TACK

Have your tack thoroughly checked by your saddler, as there is nothing so annoying as a sore back which could have been prevented, or an unnecessarily broken girth strap. How are you going to carry the essential headcollar and rope each day? What about spare shoes, or a false shoe?

What to take on the ride depends on how much back-up you have. If you have to carry a change of clothes, etc., then you are into very careful planning indeed - balance saddle bag, the lot. If you are based at your first night stop all the time, then life is much easier. You should always carry a first aid kit for horse and rider. You will also have to plan how to wash the girth and numnah. Remember our delightful climate and always carry a waterproof and additional warm clothing - it never pays to gamble with rain and wind.

SAFETY

It is always wiser to ride in company. The other person can always hold your horse, or pull you out of the ditch, as well as being someone to talk to about the excitements of the day and to help plan everything. You should always wear a BSI riding hat, properly secured, and also safe footwear. You need a clearly defined heel and a smooth sole. Even if riding in company, tell someone where you are going and roughly how long you expect to take. If affordable, take a portable telephone. Make a list of the things you must carry every day and check it before leaving base.

INSURANCE

You should have Third Party Legal Liability Insurance. This will protect you if you or your horse cause a bit of mayhem (accidentally!). Membership of the BHS gives you this type of insurance, plus Personal Accident Insurance as part of the membership package. Check your household insurance to make sure it covers riding before you rely only on that, as some insurances do not. You should always have this type of cover when venturing forth into the outside world, even if it is an hours hack from home.

PARKING

If you intend to box to the start of the day's ride, either have someone to take the box away or make sure it is safely, securely and considerately parked. If you have to make arrangements to park, do it well in advance or the contact may well have gone to market or the hairdressers when you make a last minute call. Have the vehicle number etched on to the windows for security.

MONEY

This is vital, so work out a system of getting money if necessary. Sadly we can no longer gallop up to the bank and lead Dobbin into the cashier's queue, nor do most banks have hitching rails. Post Offices are more numerous and might be a useful alternative. Always have the price of a telephone call on you.

Lastly, if you do run into problems of blocked paths or boggy ones, write to the Highway Authority of the relevant county council and tell them. Then you can do something about it. You might even think of adopting a path near home and keeping an eye on it, telling your own county council of any difficulties you encounter. It is through such voluntary work that these rides have been made possible.

Wherever you ride, always do it responsibly, with care of the land, consideration for the farmer and courtesy for all other users. Remember the Country Code and enjoy your ARROW Riding.

I hope this chapter will have started you planning and making lists. If I seem to be always writing about forward planning it is only because I usually leave things to the last minute, which causes chaos!

PHILIPPA LUARD

SOMERSET

Frequently hurried through by visitors travelling to the more well-known holiday destinations of Devon and Cornwall, Somerset remains one of the most unspoilt of English counties and thus has much to offer riders. It has a wide range of different landscapes which is due to the varied geology of the county, and an associated number of contrasting land forms. Outstanding landscape areas include the uplands of Exmoor, and the Brendon, Quantock, Mendip and Blackdown Hills. In dramatic contrast to these upland areas are the extensive, flat and low-lying levels and moors situated at the heart of the county. The remainder of Somerset is characterised by more rolling countryside fringing the uplands, or by lower ridges which interrupt the broad expanses of the Levels and Moors.

Exmoor, in the west of the county and extending into Devon, is probably the best known area of Somerset. Its national importance has been recognised by its designation, together with part of the neighbouring Brendon Hills, as a National Park. This area comprises high moorland reaching 1705 feet (520 m) at Dunkery Beacon, and deep, lush, wooded valleys. Most riders will recognise the native Exmoor ponies which graze the moors. The seaside town of Minehead is a popular resort close to Exmoor whilst Dulverton to the south provides a more rural base.

The Quantocks are a narrow range of hills, extending from near Taunton, north west for about 12 miles to the coast at Kilve, where the local geology is clearly visible in the cliffs. The hills rise to a maximum height of 1260 feet (384 m) at Will's Neck between West Bagborough and Crowcombe, which are typical of the many attractive red sandstone villages which fringe the Quantocks.

The Mendip Hills straddle the boundary of Somerset with Avon, running from Frome in the east to the coast at Weston-super-Mare, (now in Avon), in the west. The carboniferous limestone gives rise to Mendip's most spectacular natural and man-made features. Cheddar Gorge and the Wookey Hole caves, both well known popular tourist attractions, and the nearby unspoilt Ebbor Gorge, are dramatic elements of the landscape. The eastern Mendips between Shepton Mallet and Frome is one of the most intensively quarried areas in the country, accommodating two of the largest quarries in Europe. Largely developed on the plateau, they are however less visible than Battscombe Quarry at Cheddar which can be seen from many miles away. The sheltered south facing slopes around Cheddar provide an ideal environment for strawberry fields. Wells, with magnificent cathedral, is a popular tourist centre.

The Blackdown Hills lying between Taunton, Chard and Wellington, cross the county boundary into Devon. The most prominent feature is the northern escarpment, falling dramatically to the lowlands of the vale of Taunton Deane. The area is characterised by an intricate landscape of small hills and incised valleys. Blackdown villages are typically built of local chert stone, which is quite uncommon outside this area.

The Somerset Levels and Moors form the flat, low-lying area of central Somerset, extending from Glastonbury and Langport in the east, westerly along the flood plains of the Axe, Brue, Huntspill and Parrett rivers to Bridgwater Bay. The Levels comprise the coastal clay belt, whilst the Moors are overlaid with a thick deposit of peat, which is intensively worked in the Glastonbury area for the horticultural industry. Other local employment is derived from the growing of willows or 'withies' for basket making, particularly in the Athelney and Burrowbridge area. The Levels and Moors are an internationally important wetland wildlife habitat notable for wading birds and otters. Glastonbury with its abbey, and Tor which is the dominant feature in the flat landscape, is a popular tourist centre.

The gently rolling landscape of South Somerset is rich agricultural land surrounding attractive villages and small towns such as Martock and Ilchester, typically built from Ham stone quarried locally at Ham Hill. Montacute House, near Yeovil, is a National Trust property built of this attractive golden limestone. Further east, the predominantly blue-grey appearance of Langport, Somerton and surrounding villages, reflects the underlying blue lias limestone geology.

There are a wide range of sporting opportunities for riders in Somerset, which is the home of the Devon & Somerset and Quantock Staghounds, as well as a number of packs of foxhounds.

Taunton and Wincanton have racecourses which stage National Hunt meetings. Throughout the summer, agricultural and horse shows across the county provide opportunities for competition. The most prestigious is the Bath and West Show, held at the permanent showground near Shepton Mallet in late May or early June.

British Horse Society affiliated horse trials are held in the grounds of great houses such as Montacute, and Ston Eastern in the very north of the county; also at Alden, near Yeovil; Stockton Lovell, near Bridgwater; and Brendon Hills.

The Golden Horseshoe Endurance Ride is held on Exmoor each May.

Polo is played at Orchard Portman, near Taunton and at Dulverton.

Flourishing branches of the Pony Club exist for children, in every area, with similar numbers of riding clubs for adults.

CODE FOR RIDING & DRIVING RESPONSIBLY

THE BRITISH
HORSE SOCIETY

1. **Riders and carriage drivers** everywhere should proceed with courtesy, care and consideration. The British Horse Society recommends the following:

   Care for the Land
   Do not stray off the line of the path;
   Do not damage timber or hedgerows by jumping;
   Remember that horses' hooves can damage surfaces in bad weather;
   Pay particular attention to protected areas that have significant historical and/or biological value, as they are extremely sensitive to damage.

   Courtesy to other users
   Remember that walkers, cyclists and other riders may be elderly, disabled, children or simply frightened of horses; whenever possible acknowledge courtesy shown by drivers of motor vehicles.

   Consideration for the farmer
   Shut the gate behind you;
   Ride slowly past all stock;
   Do not ride on cultivated land unless the right of way crosses it;
   Dogs are seldom welcome on farmland or moorland unless on a lead or under close control.

2. **Observe local byelaws**

3. **Ride or drive with care on the roads** and take the BHS Riding and Road Safety Test. Always make sure that you can be seen at night or in bad visibility, by wearing the right kind of reflective/ fluorescent aids.

4. **Groups from riding establishments** should contain reasonable numbers, for reasons of both safety and amenity. They should never exceed twenty in total **including** the relevant number of escorts as indicated in BHS guidelines on levels of capability among riders in groups, available on request. Rides should not deviate from the right of way or permitted route and regard must be shown at all times for growing crops, shutting and securing of gates and the consideration and courtesy due to others.

5. **Always obey the Country Code in every way possible:**
   Enjoy the countryside and respect its life and work
   Guard against all risk of fire
   Fasten all gates
   Keep your dogs under close control
   Keep to public paths across farmland
   Use gates and stiles to cross fences, hedges and walls
   Leave livestock, crops and machinery alone
   Take your litter home
   Help keep all water clean
   Protect wildlife, plants and trees
   Take special care on country roads
   Make no unnecessary noise.

SOMERSET
ON HORSEBACK

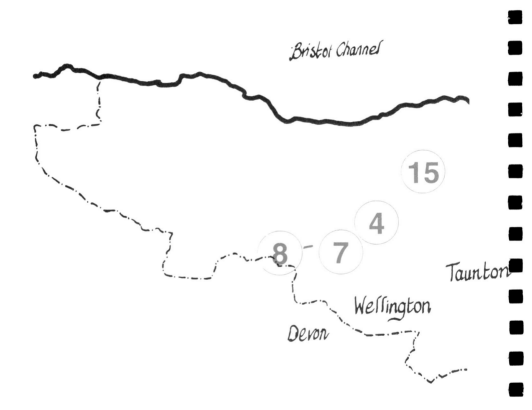

Bristol Channel

15

4

8 7

Taunton

Wellington

Devon

Avon

6

5 — Cheddar

Wells

Frome

Bridgwater

Street

Wiltshire

3 2

13

1 Wincanton

Yeovil

9 10 11 Dorset

14 12 Crewkerne

CORTON DENHAM

TRAIL 1

A 10 MILE CIRCULAR TRAIL (FIGURE OF EIGHT RIDE)

Ordnance Survey Maps:
Pathfinder: 1260
Landranger: 183

Parking & Starting Point:
Parking is available at the Queens Arms Public House, Corton Denham by prior arrangement (telephone: 0963 220317). at GR.635225. This is also your starting point.

Of Interest:

This ride has an abundance of lovely views from the high ridges but not many parking spots as the road work is all on quiet lanes with few verges, typical of Somerset. It is an area of many pretty, quiet villages, full of character, but not a Mcdonalds in sight!

Note: RUPP - Road Used as a Public Path

Route Description:

From the Queens Arms Public House (GR.635225), ride along the lane north out of Corton Denham and after approximately one mile take the first turn right which is signposted to Whitcombe Farm, and go steeply up Corton Hill at the Beacon. At the next T-junction, which is about one mile further on, cross straight over and go through the right hand gate into a field riding uphill with a wall on the left (GR.642228). Continue across two fields, keeping the hedge side to your

left to come to a gate. *Take care in the second field as there may be badger holes.* **Go through the gate and onto a track and follow the track for about 60 yards to a lane, (GR.646223). Staying to the left of the lane, continue along until you reach the next road junction.** *The very pretty valley to your right is Seven Wells Down.*

At this road junction (B3145), TAKE CARE, cross straight over and go through the gate slightly to your left onto a RUPP over Milborne Down. *The track is very obvious.* **After the first gate, stay to the side of the hedge on your left and ride along this nice long, very wide RUPP. After approximately one mile, turn right at crossroads onto another RUPP (GR.660204) for about 0.25 miles and bear round to the right as the track sweeps to the right, then immediately turn right through the gate onto Poynington Ridge, as the RUPP continues downhill.**

Ride all the way along the top of the ridge, known as Ladies Mile. *There are glorious views all around, particularly of the little village of Poyntington below, which boasts a very attractive church, but no shop or public house.* **After about 0.75 miles, where the hedge juts out in front of you, with a metal gate on your right, bear steeply downhill to your left, through the gap adjacent to a wooden gate and on through a narrower field. Go through the next gate and a shallow ford to the B3145 road junction**

(GR.647212). Cross the road and go through the gate directly opposite, to cross Poyntington Down via a steep field, staying to the left side hedge and passing through a gateway into the next field, where again the bridleway travels by the side of the stream on your left hand side, at the edge of a bracken and reed area. Go through a small gate, then diagonally right to a gate under a brick bridge. Pass under the bridge to emerge on a wide grass verge and a small metalled lane (GR.641217).

Bear right on the lane and then go immediately left to ride down Wheatsheaf Hill, signposted Corton Denham, to a triangle, and turn left, signposted to Sandford Orcas. Take the next right turn at a triangle (Staffords Green GR.632215) then go up hill on a surfaced RUPP to the top of Windmill Hill and turn right into a much narrower enclosed bridleway. Continue to ride along the top of Corton Ridge keeping on the west side of the hedge and fence, passing first Middle Ridge Lane and then Ridge Lane, going off to your right. Continue along the top of the ridge which soon drops sharply downhill to a small gate on your left. Go through the gate and into a high-hedged bridleway, and ride for about 100 yards to come to a road (GR.628242).

From the ridge the views to the west are amazing, with all the villages for miles around laid out below. Glastonbury Tor is easily picked out on the horizon, along with the Mendip mast and many other landmarks.

Turn left along the road, signposted Sutton Montis, and ride downhill to the village. At the next junction,

TRAIL 1

(GR.621241), turn left and take the next left turn, signposted Sutton Farm. Follow this semi-metalled RUPP staying on the left side of the track with waymarks to come to some farm buildings. Continue on the RUPP, as signed, to the left, going through a gate into a field and riding straight ahead as the ground rises very steeply to come to the next gate. Go through this gate and continue straight on along the side of the hill to the next gate, which is waymarked, then ride diagonally to your right going uphill to a gate leading onto Ridge Lane which is at the top of Corton Ridge. Go through this gate and down Ridge Lane (a bridleway), to turn right at the junction. Continue along this lane through the village of Corton Denham, to return to the Queens Arms, and your starting point.

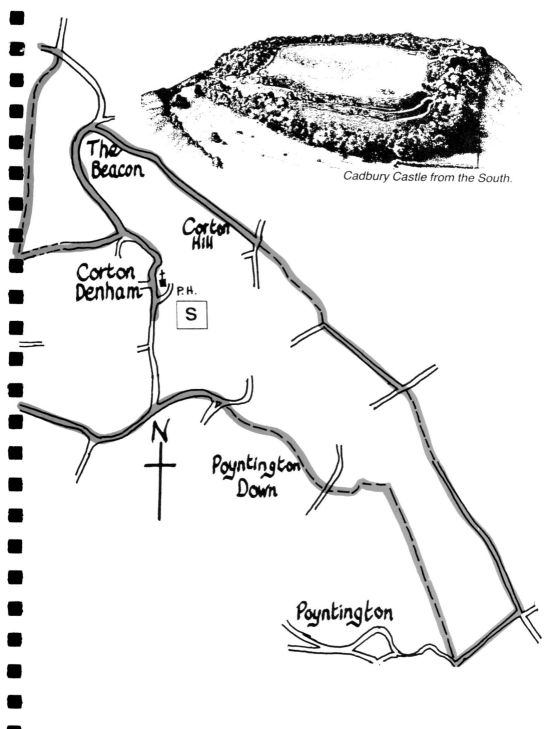

Cadbury Castle from the South.

The Beacon

Corton Hill

Corton Denham

P.H.

S

N

Poyntington Down

Poyntington

BRUTON &
KEINTON MANDEVILLE

A 26 MILE CIRCULAR TRAIL
(CLOCKWISE)

Ordnance Survey Maps:
Landranger: 183
Pathfinder: 1239 & 1259

Parking & Starting Point:
Parking is available in the Car Park at Castle Cary RailwayStation(GR.635335).

Note: RUPP - Road Used as a Public Path

Route Description:

Turn right out of the car park and ride for about 50 yards down the road. Take the only turning on the right into an unmarked track which has two cottages to the right and a yard to the left. At the end of the track, just before the railway line, follow the signed bridleway between the River Brue and the railway line to Wyke Road (GR.657340).

Turn left passing Wyke House on your right. Continue to ride through Wyke Champflower towards Bruton to fork left up a track (GR.664349) and at the crossroads turn right, then turn left and left again to follow the RUPP across Chorley Hill (GR.673353). Follow the RUPP, which is often muddy, along the valley to a ford.

Cross the ford, staying to the right, and continue along the track to a T-junction. Turn right and go through the next ford, turning left into it and right out of it, then turn left along Providence Place (West End Bruton).

Turn left and ride for 20 yards to meet the A359 at the bottom of the town of Bruton. Turn right, ride along this road for 30 yards and then turn right after the garage building but before Bees Supermarket and petrol pumps and ride up a steep incline. Ride along this track to the Mill on the Brue Holiday Centre (GR.680347). The bridleway runs through the old golf course and to the North of Gants Mill and ends at a T-junction with a lane. *Wyke Champflower lies to the right and Cole to the left.*

(Bruton)
"Priory House": a late 15th cent. half-timbered jettied town house; the stone screen was added in the 18th century.

Patwell Pump. (Bruton)

18

Turn left and go under the railway bridge to a T-junction in Cole (GR.668337). Turn right and ride through the hamlet of Cole and take the first track to Hadspen. Ride straight on at a cross tracks to meet the A359 to the north of Hadspen House (GR.662316). Cross the A359 towards Shepton Montague and ride to a T-junction. *If you wish to visit The Montague Inn, a small Public House in Shepton Montague, for refreshment, turn left at the T-junction.* At the T-junction, turn right and continue riding past Welham Farm, up Cattle Hill and then cross over the main road (A371) (GR.668298). *CARE, this is a busy road.* Take the second turn right, just after Fishermans Hut, and continue riding on to the centre of Yarlington. At the crossroads in the centre of Yarlington, turn right in front of the church into the Stag's Head car park. Ride through the car park keeping the church on your right, to Manor Farm.

Ride through the farm, bending right to Sleight Lane, a RUPP, (GR.655295). You will pass through several gates on this RUPP finally meeting a crossroads with a green lane (GR.648302). Ride straight on to meet a T-junction at a metalled road. Turn right towards Smallway and cross over the A359. Branch right and ride on for approximately 100 yards along the B3152 and take the next left turn down Cockhill Lane (GR.637310).

Dovecot: this 15th cent. tower was one of the first properties of the National Trust.
(Bruton)

Turn right down the first track on the left before the lane goes steeply downhill. *This track is known as Thornymarsh Lane and is approximately 1.50 miles long.* Keep to the left where the track divides and continue riding on to meet the railway line. *There is a telephone here where you must tell the station at Cary that you are about to cross the line to North Barrow (GR.619299).* Cross the railway line and take the next turn left to North Barrow and ride on to meet Barrow Lane at a T-junction just west of a railway bridge.

Turn right and continue to ride through North Barrow to the crossroads known as Barrow Cross (GR.604294). Turn left and proceed for 100 yards before turning right into Bills Lane. Follow this bridleway until it joins the metalled road (GR.562279).

(Bruton)
St Mary's Church; one of Somerset's finest Perpendicular churches, with two towers and a classical chancel.

19

Turn right and proceed for 0.50 miles to the Red Lion Public House. *Horses can be tethered here and refreshment obtained.* On leaving the Red Lion car park, turn right and ride straight ahead, ignoring the turnings left into Babcary and right to Foddington. Cross the ford (GR.565292) and keep left on the bridleway (Westover Lane). *TAKE GREAT CARE when you cross the Fosse Way (A37) at GR.558294).* Follow the bridleway, known as Babcary Lane, north into Keinton Mandeville.

Cross over the main road (B3153) in Keinton Mandeville and into Cottons Lane opposite. Turn into the first field gate on the right (GR.553313) and follow the unmarked bridleway for about one mile into West Lydford.

At West Lydford turn left, cross the bridge over the River Brue and take the first turning to the left, about 150 yards past West Lydford Church. Keeping left on this bridleway, following the river, go through an iron gate (GR.562322). The bridleway then turns right, heading north, across an open field to Southwood Cover.

Go through a wicket gate into Southwood Cover. Follow the track through the Southwood Cover and over a concrete bridge over a water course, through another open field to Southwood (GR.558334).

Cross the metalled road and proceed north on Middle Drove which passes between Southwood House and Southwood Farm. At the T-junction turn right and at the next T-junction turn left on to Back Lane, which is a metalled road.

At the next T-junction, turn right into Ham Street. Turn left at the next T-junction at Lottisham House and 150 yards further on turn right into an unmarked bridleway known as Lottisham Lane.

At the end of Lottisham Lane, turn right on to a metalled road. Pass Stone Farm on the left and cross the Fosse Way (A37) WITH CARE (GR.584338).

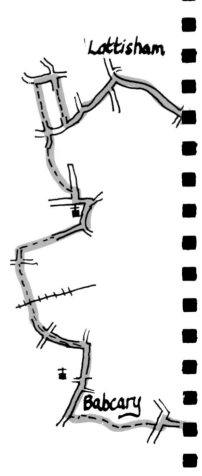

Leaving Homblotton Church on the right, go straight through Easton town and follow the unmarked bridleway through fields to the ancient stone Bolter's Bridge (GR.607334). Cross the bridge and follow the clearly defined bridleway to the metalled road at Sutton. Keeping right, follow the road to Brook House Inn (GR.634340). Turn right on the busy main road (A371) and proceed south for 500 yards to Castle Cary Railway Station and your parking place.

The 15th cent. Packhorse Bridge (BRUTON)

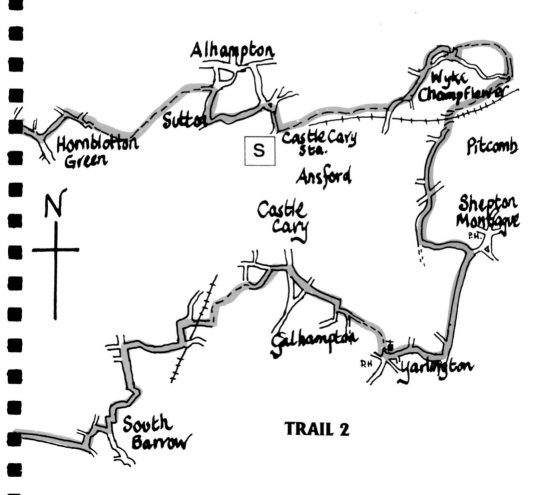

TRAIL 2

AROUND CASTLE CARY

TRAIL 3

A 11 MILE CIRCULAR TRAIL (CLOCKWISE)

Ordnance Survey Maps:
Landranger: 183
Pathfinder: 1239 & 1260

Parking & Starting Points:
Parking is available at The Harvester Public House, Galhampton (GR.635299) by prior arrangement. Please telephone (0963) 440510. Your ride is described from here.

Parking Note:
It is also possible to park at Castle Cary Railway Station (GR.635336), which can accommodate transport and trailers.

Of Interest:
It is intended that this should be a half-day ride. This ride, which encircles the village of Castle Cary, brings to the rider a tremendous variety of scenery and terrain, from the water meadows along the River Brue to the hidden valleys and combes of Knap Hollow and Hadspen, to say nothing of the spectacular views to be had across the Brue Valley and on to Glastonbury Tor; or the view across to Alfred's Tower and Pen Selwood which lie on the opposite hillside.

Route Description:

From your parking place at The Harvester Public House, turn immediately left and ride down Long Street. Continue on bearing left down hill to the triangle and then left into Frog Lane where you ride along the road and past a farm, up to a barn with a lane intersecting on the right.

Continue up the road until it meets the A359. *CARE this is a busy road.* Cross straight over into Small Way Lane and ride on to meet the B3152. Turn right towards Castle Cary. After approximately 250 yards, turn left at the signpost to Cock Hill, then after a further 250 yards turn left again into Thorney Marsh Lane. *This lane winds down the hill, not quite as steeply as Cock Hill, through a leafy track which, as the name implies, can sometimes be boggy.* Take the only right hand turning along this RUPP going back towards Cockhill Lane. Turn right and ride for a short distance before turning into the entrance of Cockhill Farm. Ride straight through the farmyard and through the cattle yard *(in winter this may be full of cattle!).*

Carry straight on along the track known as Maggs Lane. Pass the Sewage Works on the right and turn right when reaching the road (GR.627319). *The track here now becomes a road running alongside the River Cary.* Pass the Dimmer Bridge then continue to Fulford's Cross, then turn left over the railway bridge and ride along Blackworthy Road to join the B3153 at Clanville. Turn right here and continue to Station Road, which goes over the railway line. THIS STRETCH OF ROAD IS BUSY SO TAKE GREAT CARE. Ride on to pass the Railway Station on the right. Just past a row of cottages, cross the road and turn right down a surfaced track (GR.635336). Pass the

TRAIL 3

St. John's Priory

Castle Cary

The Market House

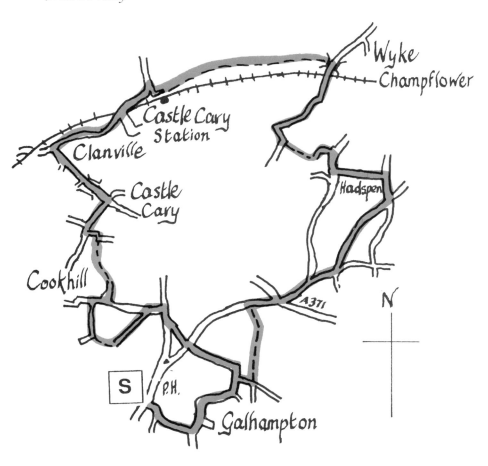

back of houses heading towards a footbridge over the railway line and then bear left on the track keeping the railway line on the right and the yard on the left.

Ride across the centre of the field, halfway across bear slightly left towards a gap in the opposite hedge. Go through the gap and into the next large field and bear left to a hunting gate. Near the end of the next very large field, ride towards the hedge at the left corner and go through the adjoining bridlegate and straight across the field to another bridlegate adjacent to the barn. Go through the next bridlegate and into the last field, across to a gate and out onto the Wyke Road (GR.657340). Turn right and follow the road, first crossing the railway bridge. Continue along Wyke Road, which is a pleasant country lane, for nearly a mile. *Enjoy the spectacular views back across the Brue Valley.*

After the road makes a sharp, right-angled turn to the left, look for the bridleway waymarker about 120 yards on the left. Turn left (GR.651330) and go through the gate onto the bridleway

which is in a field. Ride steeply down hill to the left-hand corner, which is wooded, to come to a gate. Go through the gate. The track turns to the left and becomes boggy in places. Continue following the obvious track until the Cole-Hadspen road is reached (GR.657329). Turn right along the road towards Hadspen, then take the first turn left signposted Nettlescombe Hill, going steeply uphill and becoming a rough lane.

When you meet a T-junction of tracks at Ridge Lane, turn right and shortly after turn right again at Stumps Cross crossroads. Ride along this road until you meet Bruton Road (GR.657315). Turn right here and continue to the crossroads where you ride straight over towards Yeovil and the A359. After about 120 yards, turn left at a bridlegate leading into a field. Keeping the hedge on the right, follow the bridleway down through two fields to Hicks Lane. Turn right here and continue along to meet Frog Lane where you retrace your steps back to the triangle, uphill bearing right to Long Street and so back to your parking place at The Harvester Public House.

Castle Cary

24

BRIDLEWAYS

HOW TO FIND YOURS

There are many miles of rights of way throughout the country on which you may ride: these fall into three types: they are Bridleways, Byways Open to All Traffic and Unclassified County Roads (which may be referred to as field roads or green lanes).

MAPS

The best maps to use while riding are the Ordnance Survey 1:25,000 (2.5" to the mile) Maps since these show the field boundaries. The maps of this scale, known as the Pathfinder Series, show Bridleways as a line of green dashes.

The Rights of Way information shown on a printed map was correct at the time that the map was printed but changes do take place: if you have any reason to query the Rights of Way information on a printed map it will be necessary for you to consult the Definitive Map and the County Council Rights of Way Officer to resolve the query.

The Definitive Map is a legal document held and maintained by the County Council; copies may also be found at County Council Area/Local/Divisional Offices and Parish Clerks'Offices and local libraries. The Definitive Maps are available for inspection by any member of public who wishes to see them. It would be a courtesy to telephone and ask for the relevant sheets to be made available.

**THE BRITISH
HORSE SOCIETY**

ASH COMMON

TRAIL 4

A 15 MILE CIRCULAR TRAIL (CLOCKWISE)

Ordnance Survey Maps:
Landrangers: 193 & 181
Pathfinders: 1246 & 1257

Parking & Starting Points:
Parking is available on Ash Common (GR.152289) which is situated approximately one mile west of the A358 at Bishops Lydeard. Ash Common is also your starting point.

NOTE:
RUPP - Road Used as a Public Path
UCR - Unclassified County Road

Of Interest:
This route takes in the parishes of Ash Priors, Halse, Fitzhead, Tolland and Lydeard St Lawrence.

Route Description:

From Ash Common (GR.152289), follow the RUPP south-east to Stallenge Farm (GR.157277), riding on through the ford to a UCR where you turn right (GR.155274). Continue straight on until you reach the village of Halse. Turn left to the village and hall and then turn right (GR.144276) onto a RUPP.

Turn left off the RUPP onto a UCR and follow this to take the next turning on the left, continuing on towards Milverton.

Turn right (GR.126264) onto a RUPP towards River Farm. At the end of the track, turn right and then left (GR.119273) onto another RUPP. Turn left off this track (GR.113275) onto a UCR and after approximately 200 yards, turn sharp right (GR.111275).

Leave this RUPP at GR.113282, going onto a road. Follow the road leaving Knights Farm on your left, then turn left at the next road junction and continue on past Burrow Hill Farm. Take the next turn right (GR.109301) and then the next left (GR.110302).

Ride on leaving Scarr Chapel on your right and then take the next bridleway on your right through a white gate (GR.105306) onto Watersmeet Farm. Continue straight on riding through the ford to Gaulden Manor (GR.112315).

Turn left onto a UCR (GR.122315) and take the next turn right to Grove Farm. Continue on to meet a road and turn left (GR.114325). Take the next turn right to Cheese Dairy. At Cheese Dairy, turn right (GR.119328) onto a RUPP and continue along here to meet a road.

At the road, turn left (GR.120318) passing a filling station and take the next turn left towards Lydeard St Lawrence. At the end of this track, turn right, then take the first turning on the left and continue leaving the Friendship Public House on your left (GR.131314). Take the second turn right to Pitpear Farm. Ride through the farmyard and at the first gate on the left, turn onto a bridleway to Denbury Farm.

Follow this bridleway to Ash Priors. At Park Gate House, turn right onto a UCR and follow this track back to your starting place.

GAULDEN MANOR. Tolland

Lydeard St. Lawrence

Tolland

PH

TRAIL 4

Hoccombe

N

Ash Priors

S

Fitzhead

PH

Halse

Preston Bowyer

TRAIL
5

A 10 MILE CIRCULAR TRAIL (ANTI-CLOCKWISE)

Ordnance Survey Maps:
Landranger: 182
Pathfinder: 1198

Parking & Starting Points:
Parking is available between Tynings Gate and Ashridge Farm, or on the side of the road at Tynings Farm (GR.470565) which is your starting point.

NOTE: Although there is some road work on this route, it is all along quiet back streets and in a very picturesque area.

Of Interest:
At the beginning of Middledown Drove, there is a second bridleway gate on your right. This trail goes back to Batcombe Hollow and Batcombe Farm to Top Road. If you turn right, you can return to Cheddar via Bradley Cross.

Route Description:

From Tynings Farm (GR.470565) ride south-west down an old cart track known as Warrens Hill Road. When you come to open land and a hedge, turn left and then almost immediately right and continue riding along the track to a gate. Go through the gate and onto a road (GR.457542).

Turn right and ride along the road for approximately 25 yards. *Watch out for lorries on this road.* Turn left into Hannay Road and then left into Kent Street, passing the Kings Head and the Gardiners Arms Public Houses.

Continue straight on to Birch Hill Road and ride on down to the Butchers Arms. Here, turn left and go over the stream. *If you would like to look at Cheddar Gorge, and your horse is good in traffic, follow the road up through the village.* After you have crossed the bridge over the stream, turn right at the Gonglis Craft Village and bear left continuing up hill. This road continues into Bradley Cross Lane.

At Bradley Cross there is a post box set back on the left and a white cottage. Keep to the right of the cottage and follow the track waymarked 'Draycott'. You are now on an old bridleway which continues until you get to Middledown Drove just above Corselift Farm. Follow this Drove until you get to the B3135 near Cheddar Head and cross the road. Continue toward Kingdown Farm. At the crossroads, turn left, going north, towards Charterhouse and past Warren Farm riding over the 'lead' mineries. Pass the church and then ride straight over at the crossroads to the next road, a marked bridleway called Rains Batch. *This bridleway takes you past the masts of the wireless station.* Keeping the masts on your right, follow the track until you get to Blackdown. Follow the main track between high 'mole hills'; *these were used to stop aircraft landing during the war.* Take the next track on the left, leading south, and ride past a bunker and through the gate. You will now be able to see Tynings Farm and your starting place.

TRAIL 5

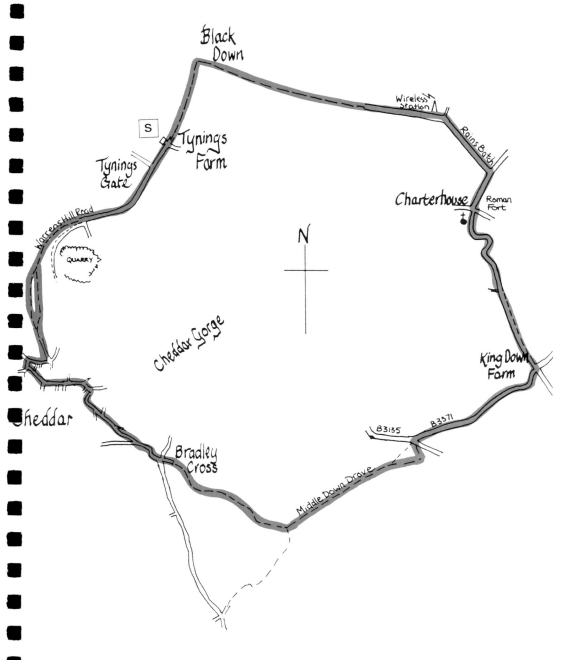

Black Down

Wireless Station

Rains Batch

Tynings Farm

S

Tynings Gate

Charterhouse

Roman Fort

Warrens Hill Road

QUARRY

N

Cheddar Gorge

King Down Farm

Cheddar

B3135

B3371

Bradley Cross

Middle Down Drove

ROWBERROW & BURRINGTON

A 7 MILE CIRCULAR TRAIL (CLOCKWISE)

Ordnance Survey Maps:
Landranger: 182
Pathfinder: 1198

Parking & Starting Point:
Parking is available at Tynings Farm (GR.470566) on the good roadside verge. Tynings Farm is on the Charterhouse to Shipham road. This is also your starting point.

Route Description:

From Tynings Farm ride in a westerly direction following the West Mendip Way, via Hollow Rock, a water pumping station and so on down to Rowberrow Bottom. Ride past a number of cottages, the last of which is pink, and follow the bridleway through woods until you come to a T-junction (GR.453584). Turn right heading east and follow this old track for about one mile when you meet a rough tarmac track. Continue on downhill to the village of Burrington and the B3134 road (GR.477591). *If you wish to take refreshments, turn right here, and pass the Garden Centre and visit the public house, next door, which offers good fare and a hitching rail for your horses. You can also see the 'Rock of Ages'. After your refreshments return to the junction with the B3134.*

Cross over the B3134 on to a minor road and after about 0.25 miles you will meet two bridleways. Take either of these tracks and ride across Burrington Ham until you reach a metalled road at a car park. *You may find an ice-cream van here!* Turn left at this road (B3134) (GR.490581). After riding for about 50 yards, turn right on to a bridleway taking you by Ellick Farm and to Black Down. In a short distance you will see three tracks ahead. Take any one of these to ride over the Down and so back to Tynings Farm and your starting point.

Chapel & pond at Rickford

TRAIL 6

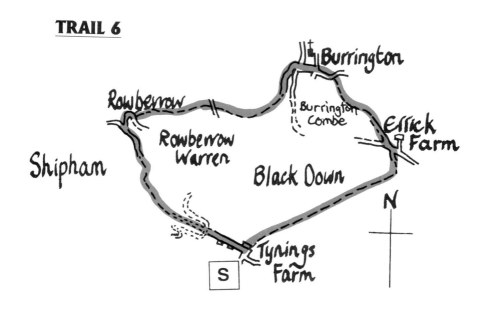

A view from the Mendip Hills

31

WASHBATTLE BRIDGE

AN 8 MILE CIRCULAR TRAIL (ANTI-CLOCKWISE)

Ordnance Survey Maps:
Pathfinder: 1257
Landranger: 181

Parking & Starting Points:
Parking is available at The Barn by prior arrangement. Please telephone (0984) 624206. There may be a small charge for parking. This is also your starting point (GR.048286).

Of Interest:
There are some beautiful views along this route with little traffic. Unfortunately there are no 'watering holes' for riders so you would be advised to take your own refreshment with you.

Route Description:

From your parking place, take the very pretty, quiet Huish Cleeve Road going west. Follow this road up hill passing Huish Cleeve and Hart's Path Plantations on the left and New Plantation on the right. Where the road goes sharply to the right, alongside New Plantation, turn sharp left along the gated bridleway. Ride along this track to come to a gate leading onto a road (GR.023280). Go through the gate and turn left and in a short distance turn right along Old Way. Follow this lane for about 0.75 miles and then take the bridleway on the right (GR.036272) to Raddington Bottom, going through several gates along the track.

TRAIL 7

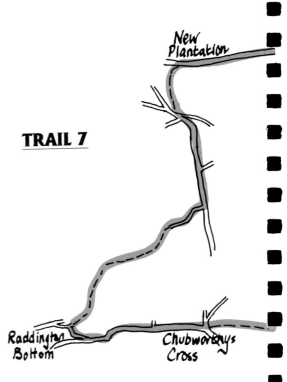

When you reach Raddington Bottom, turn left and then left again onto a road to Chubworthy Cross where you will come to a T-junction (GR.026262). Cross straight over and ride down the bridleway to Chipstable Farm. Here you will meet a road. Turn left along the road towards Crooks Farm. Before you reach the farm you will come to a road junction. Take the right hand lane and then turn sharp right onto the bridleway (GR.044270) which becomes Pitt Lane and leads down to Wadham's Farm and Marshes Farm.

At the junction of tracks at Marshes Farm, take the bridleway on the left (GR.055264) and follow this track over Bulland Ford and alongside the River Tone to Washbattle Bridge. Take the road across the bridge going uphill. Pass Newhouse Farm and turn left at Tanners Corner, signposted 'Huish Moor', and so back to your starting point.

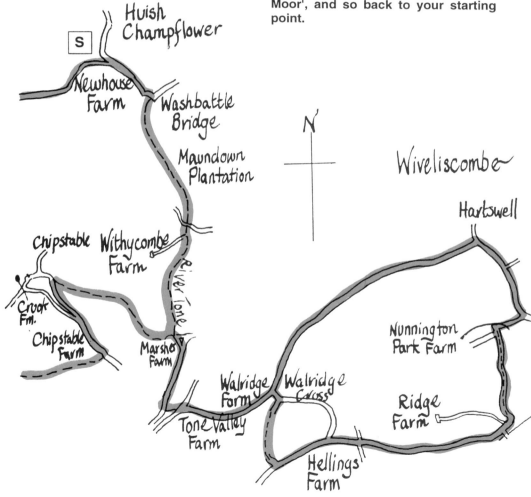

TRAIL
8

A 9 MILE CIRCULAR TRAIL
(ANTI-CLOCKWISE)

Ordnance Survey Maps:
Pathfinder: 1257
Landranger: 181

Parking & Starting Points:
Parking is available at The Barn by prior arrangement. Please telephone (0984) 624206. There may be a small charge for parking. This is also your starting point (GR.048286)

NOTE: Although there is quite a lot of road work on this trail, it is all along quiet lanes with little traffic.

RUPP - Road Used as a Public Path.

Route Description:

From your parking place take the Huish Cleeve road going east to a T-junction at Tanners Corner where you turn right. Follow this road past Newhouse Farm and take the road across Washbattle Bridge (GR.053286). From Washbattle Bridge, take the track alongside the River Tone to Bulland Ford. Cross the ford and go half-left along bridleway to Wadhams Farm. Keep riding left through the farm yard and so on to the road to Waterrow. *Here you will find the Rock Inn, the landlord is very welcoming to all callers.*

Cross the road, go left over the bridge and in a short distance turn right along the narrow Spears Lane to pass Tone Valley Farm on the right. At the end of

Spears Lane, having passed Walridge Farm on the left, you will come to Walridge Cross where you turn right. Ride along the lane for a very short distance and where Bicking's Close Lane goes off to the left, you turn right onto the RUPP towards Hellings Farm.

When you reach a T-junction at the end of the RUPP, turn left along the narrow country lane and pass Hellings Farm on the right. Stay on this lane until just before reaching the railway bridge over a disused line where you fork left to take the RUPP north. *This track is known as Quarthill Lane.* Ride on along this lane passing Nunnington Park Farm on the right and further along, Higher Nunnington Farm on the left. Turn left at the next T-junction onto a road. Ride along this road for approximately 0.75 miles and then turn left into Pyncombe Lane.

Follow Pyncombe Lane until you reach Walridge Cross where you turn right, back into Spears Lane with Walridge Farm now on your right.

Retrace your steps from Waterrow back through the farm yard at Wadhams Farm and alongside the River Tone to Washbattle Bridge. Take the road across the bridge going uphill. Pass Newhouse Farm and turn left at Tanners Corner, signposted 'Huish Moor', and so return to your starting point.

TRAIL 8

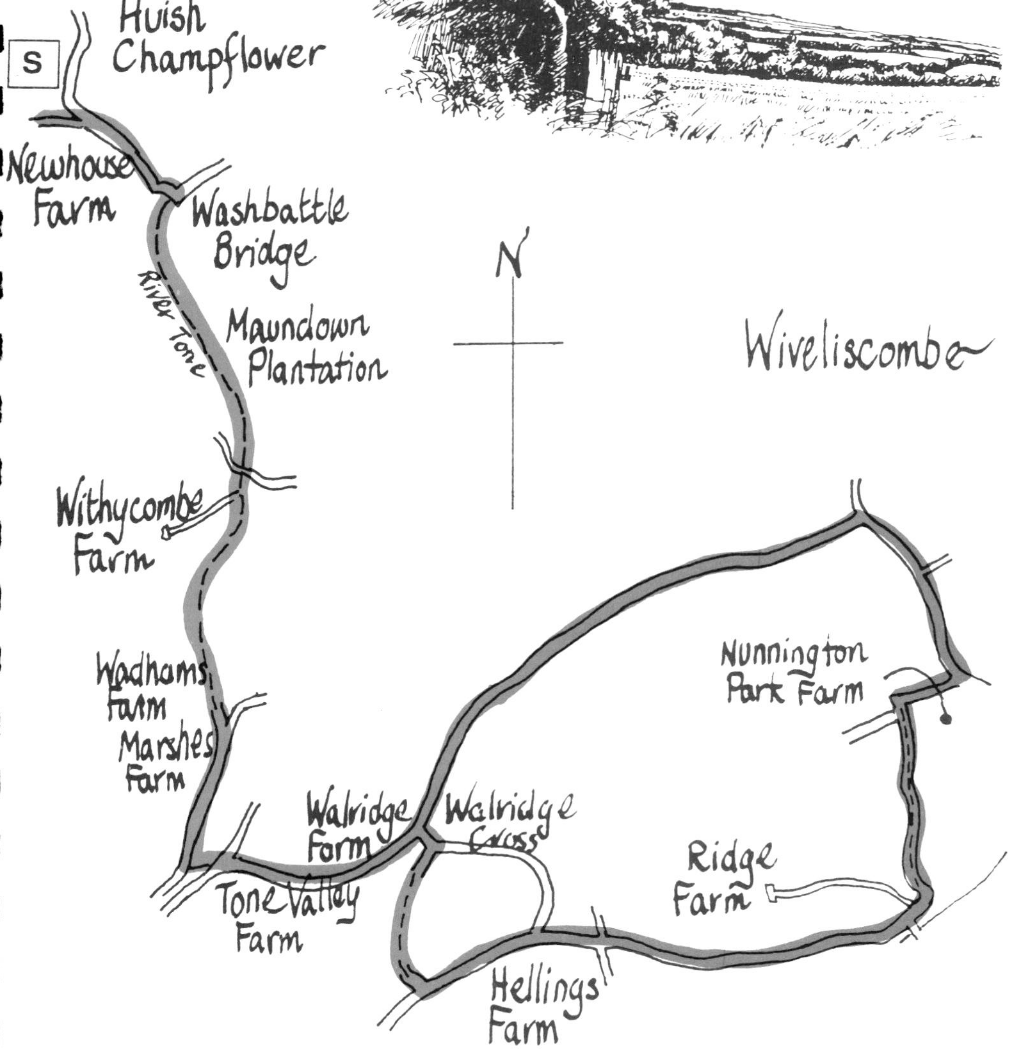

Huish Champflower

S

Newhouse Farm

Washbattle Bridge

River Tone

Maundown Plantation

N

Wiveliscombe

Withycombe Farm

Wadhams Farm

Marshes Farm

Nunnington Park Farm

Walridge Farm

Walridge Cross

Ridge Farm

Tone Valley Farm

Hellings Farm

FOLLOWING A ROUTE

The descriptions given in this
book were correct at the time of
printing but it should be borne in
mind that landmarks and
conditions can change.
It is assumed every user will
carry and be competent in the
use of the appropriate Ordnance
Survey Pathfinder or
Landranger map. This is
essential as the route may not
be waymarked along the whole
of its length.

THE HARDINGTON MANDEVILLE TRAILS

The Hardington Mandeville Trails are a collection of three rides varying in length from 6.50 miles to 12 miles, around the Parish of Hardington Mandeville. They all start at the same place and therefore give the rider the opportunity to either lengthen or shorten their route according to the day. On each of the rides the first four miles are on road. However, this is usually very quiet and there are good verges all the way along Common Lane.

The following information is common to each of the three rides:

Ordnance Survey Maps:
Pathfinder: 1279 & 1298
Landrangers: 193 & 194

Parking & Starting Points:
Parking for all three rides is available in Hardington Mandeville at the bottom of Windmill Hill (GR.512114) which is also the starting point of the description of all the rides.

PARKING NOTE: To locate the wide verge at the bottom of Windmill Hill, head south from St Mary's Church and take the second left turn towards Penn House Farm and Pen Hill Farm. The verge is immediately on the right. Parking is also available at Pendomer (GR.524107) on the wide grass verge on the left side of the road leading to Pendomer.

Of Interest:
These rides offer fine views of the Somerset and Dorset countryside and take you through a variety of small and attractive country roads, lanes, fields and woodland.
Hardington *is an Anglo-Saxon name and means 'the settlement of Hearda's people'. In 1086 the Manor belonged to the king who later handed it over to Geoffrey de Mandeville. Hardington is divided into three parts. The largest is usually referred to as 'the Mandeville' and contains the medieval church which was largely rebuilt in the 19th Century, (although part of the Norman tower remains), The Mandeville Arms public house and the High Street (which has no shops!).*
Hardington Moor, *is in the valley of the Chinnock Brook to the north, where there is another pub, The Royal Oak, and the village shop and Post Office.*
Hardington Marsh *is a mile away to the south and just a handful of farms and dwellings down a 'No Through Road'.*
Pendomer *lies east of Hardington Marsh overlooking Pen Wood - a delightful little hamlet with a Norman church.*
Pen Wood *covers 240 acres of Birt Hill rising 600 feet above sea level on the Somerset/Dorset border. The wood is privately owned and is managed as a commercial working forest. A Nature Trail has been established by the South Somerset District Council in co-operation with the wood's owner and is a haven for wildlife.*

HARDINGTON MANDEVILLE I

TRAIL 9

A 6.50 MILE CIRCULAR TRAIL (ANTI-CLOCKWISE)

Route Description:

From you parking place at the bottom of Windmill Hill in Hardington Mandeville, head west for a short distance and at a crossroads, known as Hill Cross, turn left and ride down the hill keeping right at the bottom. Continue along New Road, passing the Stud and then New Plantation on your left. Ride up the hill passing East Lease Farm at the top on the left. Continue on down the next hill and at the bottom, turn left into Common Lane, signposted No Through Road. Continue along this lane to the cattle grid and go through the gate to the left hand side to access the bridleway.

Ride along the bridleway, passing a turn to the left and then through a small copse. *In a short distance you will see Kingswood Farm, set back on your left.* The track takes you through an electrically controlled gate, which is usually open, and then bends right (GR.490093). Go through the gate and turn left through another gate and across to a gate in the opposite hedge. Go through this gate keeping the hedge on your left and ride straight ahead and through a gap, or the gate, into the next field. Keep riding straight across a field, crossing a bridge over a ditch (GR.500091)and then bear slightly right towards a bridlegate in the corner of the next field, adjacent to the railway line. *Timetables for the trains should be displayed on the gates.*

Ride along the short, enclosed section below the railway line to exit at a gate into a field. Ride diagonally left away from the railway line towards trees and then through a metal gate over a bridge. Keeping the tree line on your left, enter an enclosed section through a bridlegate. *This is Shortmarsh Lane.* At the end of the enclosed section, exit via a bridlegate at Marsh Farm. Go through the farmyard and then turn left onto a road. Ride along the road. After 1.50 miles the road bends left and shortly after this you must turn right and ride up the hill. When you come to the crossroads, turn right and then right again bringing you back to your starting point.

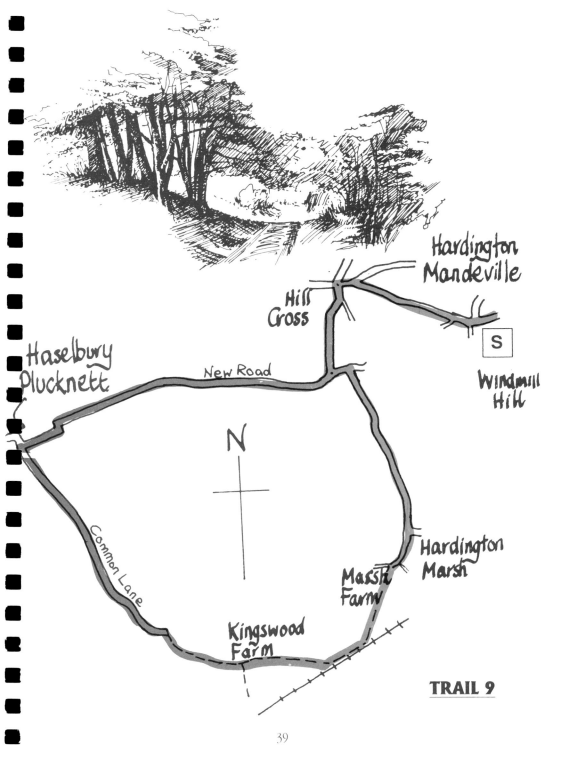

Hardington
Mandeville

Hill
Cross

Haselbury
Plucknett

New Road

S

Windmill
Hill

N

Common Lane

Hardington
Marsh

Marsh
Farm

Kingswood
Farm

TRAIL 9

TRAIL 10

A 10 MILE CIRCULAR TRAIL (ANTI-CLOCKWISE)

Route Description:

From your parking place at the bottom of Windmill Hill, head west for a short distance to turn left at Hill Cross crossroads and ride down the hill, keeping right at the bottom. Continue along New Road, passing the stud and then New Plantation on your left. Ride up the hill with East Lease Farm on the left at the top and then at the bottom of the next hill, turn left into Common Lane which is signposted No Through Road (GR.481106). Continue along the trail to the cattle grid and go through the gate on the left to access the bridleway.

Continue on, passing a left turn, and ride on through a small copse. *You will see Kingswood Farm set back on your left.* The track takes you through an electrically operated gate, but this is usually open, and then it bends right towards White Vine Farm. Ride on up the hill, over the railway bridge and through a metal gate. *Take a rest at the top and enjoy the beautiful view.* **Pass White Vine Farm on the left and then leave the track before it bends left, to go through a metal gate on the right and so into a field. Ride across the field to another metal gate opposite. Go through this gate and then ride straight ahead for a short way to turn right through a gap in the bushes to go up a narrow field with trees and gorse on either side.**

Wind your way through the copse ahead to come to a bridlegate at the top right hand corner leading you into the woods. Follow the path parallel to the field on the left at first and then veering slightly right-handed, eventually bearing left down to a bridlegate leading into a field. Go through the gate and ride up the field with the hedge on your left, to come to a gate in the opposite hedge. Go through this gate and ride with this hedge on your right to a gate in the far corner. Pass through this gate and follow the track left down to Wyke Farm. *You are now in Dorset.* **Follow this track in a clockwise direction through metal gates leaving the farm and buildings on your right. Continue on the tarmac drive up a steep hill to a cattle grid.**

At the left of the cattle grid is a bridlegate. Go through this gate and onto a tarmac road (GR.500066). *Crook Hill is on your right with Chedington Woods beyond. Toller Down is ahead on the skyline.* **Turn left along the tarmac road and ride for one mile until you come to a right hand turn signposted 'Corscombe 1 mile'. Do not turn here, but continue straight ahead to a left hand turn signposted Higher Halstock Leigh, No Through Road. Turn left and ride through a small hamlet to where the road becomes a track.** *This is actually an unclassified county road to the Dorset/ Somerset border where it becomes a* *bridleway.* Continue riding up the track and through a metal bridlegate into an enclosed section. Ride through another metal bridlegate, over a small stream and up a bank, into a field.

TRAIL 10

Keeping the copse on your left, ride across the field and through the gate. Continue with the trees on your left and go through a wide gap in the old hedgerow ahead. *Pen Wood is high up on your right.* Still with the hedge on your left, ride down the hill and veering slightly right, ride into the next field and cross the bridge over the stream.

Ride up the field to the top right hand corner. Go through the gate and along an enclosed section of bridleway. Go through a metal gate, over the railway bridge and onto a tarmac road, just before Marsh Farm. After 1.50 miles the road bends left and soon after this you must turn right and ride up the hill. At the cross roads turn right and then turn right again to return to your starting point.

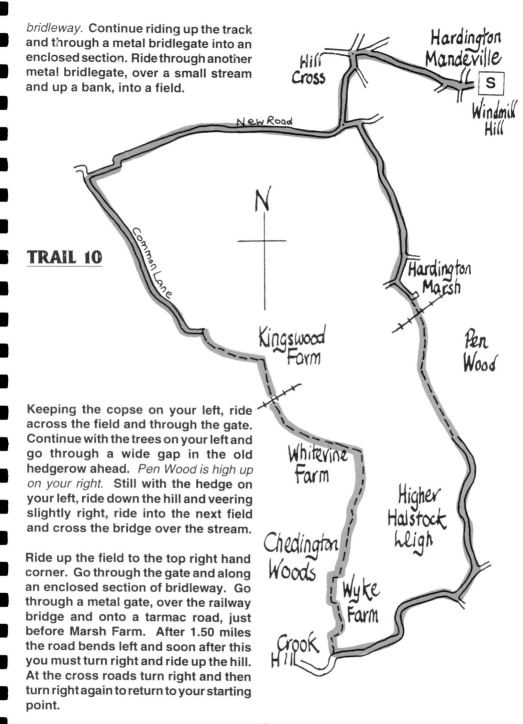

TRAIL 11

A 12 MILE CIRCULAR TRAIL (ANTI-CLOCKWISE)

Route Description:

From your parking place at the bottom of Windmill Hill, head west for a short distance to turn left at Hill Cross crossroads and ride down the hill, keeping right at the bottom. Continue along New Road, passing the stud and then New Plantation on your left. Ride up the hill with East Lease Farm on the left at the top and then at the bottom of the next hill, turn left into Common Lane which is signposted 'No Through Road' (GR.481106). Continue along the trail to the cattle grid and go through the gate on the left to access the bridleway.

Continue on past a left turn and ride on through a small copse. *You will see Kingswood Farm set back on your left.* The track takes you through an electrically operated gate, but this is usually open, and then bends right towards White Vine Farm. Ride on up the hill, over the railway bridge and through a metal gate. *Take a rest at the top and enjoy the beautiful view.* Pass White Vine Farm on the left and then leave the track before it bends left, to go through a metal gate on the right and so into a field. Ride across the field to another metal gate opposite. Go through this gate and then ride straight ahead for a short way to turn right through a gap in the bushes to go up a narrow field with trees and gorse on either side.

Wind your way through the copse ahead to come to a bridlegate at the top right hand corner leading you into the woods. Follow the path parallel to the field on the left at first and then veering slightly right handed, eventually bearing left down to a bridlegate leading into a field. Go through the gate and ride up the field with the hedge on your left, to come to a gate in the opposite hedge. Go through this gate and ride with this hedge on your right to a gate in the far corner. Pass through this gate and follow the track left down to Wyke Farm. Follow this track in a clockwise direction through metal gates leaving the farm and buildings on your right. Continue on the tarmac drive up a steep hill to a cattle grid.

At the left of the cattle grid is a bridlegate. Go through this gate and onto a tarmac road. *Crook Hill is on your right with Chedington Woods beyond. Toller Down is ahead on the skyline.* Turn left along the tarmac road and ride for one mile until you come to a right hand turn (GR.510071) signposted 'Corscombe 1 mile'.

Turn right here and ride towards Corscombe along this pretty lane which takes you steeply down, over a woodland stream and up a short, steep hill. Look for a white house on the right; just after this, there is a sharp right hand bend. **Just before the bend, turn left into an enclosed track** - *an unclassified county road.* **Ride along this track, known as Common Lane, for 1.50 miles, keeping left at a junction with another track.** *The going is wet in places, but there is a firm footing throughout. Halstock Golf course can be seen to the left.*

On reaching Halstock, turn hard left (GR.538079) onto a tarmac road. Ride past Vale Farm, which is a pink house, on your left and the Community Centre on your right. Where the road bends left to Lower Halstock Leigh, turn right, signposted Halstock Mill. Follow the road and pass signs saying 'Private' and 'No turning beyond this point'. The road which bends right is now a bridleway. Ride across the gravel drive leaving Halstock Mill on your left, and through a metal gate ahead into a wooded section.

Ride along the left side. At the end of the section you will come to a bridlegate. Go through the gate and keep straight ahead through a narrow section surrounded by trees with a field on the right. *The next section, through more trees, can be boggy.* **Keep to the left and follow the left hand hedge to double bridlegates enclosing a sleeper bridge. Keep diagonally right and ride across the field to a bridlegate and into a wood.** *Abbot's Hill is to your right with Coker Woods beyond. Pen Wood is to your left.* **Exit from the wood through a bridlegate and into a field. Keeping the hedge on your right, ride to a gate at the top right hand corner and into an enclosed section. At the end of this section, go through the metal gate and into a field heading for the railway line with Parsonage Farm on your right. Go through the gate on**

the right near the embankment. Cross the yard leaving the barn on your right, bear left under the railway bridge and continue right towards Pendomer. *Pen Wood Forest Trail is to the left after the railway bridge - no dogs or horses are allowed on this trail.*

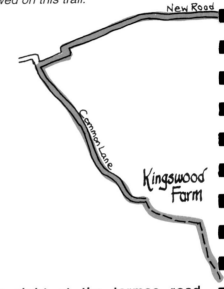

Turn right at the tarmac road (GR.524106) with Rose Cottage on the right. Ride up Pendomer Road. *If you wish to start your ride from Pendomer, the right hand verge is a possible parking place.* **When you come to a road junction, turn left and left again at Pen Cross where there is a large stone house on the left. Continue to ride along this road which is usually quiet and has some good verges. Pass Pen Hill Farm on the left and then on the right Pen House Farm followed by Prospect Farm.** *There are far reaching views of the West Somerset Hills ahead, Coker Hill to the right and Pen Wood to the left with Toller Down on the skyline beyond.*

Ride on down the hill to find your starting place at the bottom on the left hand side.

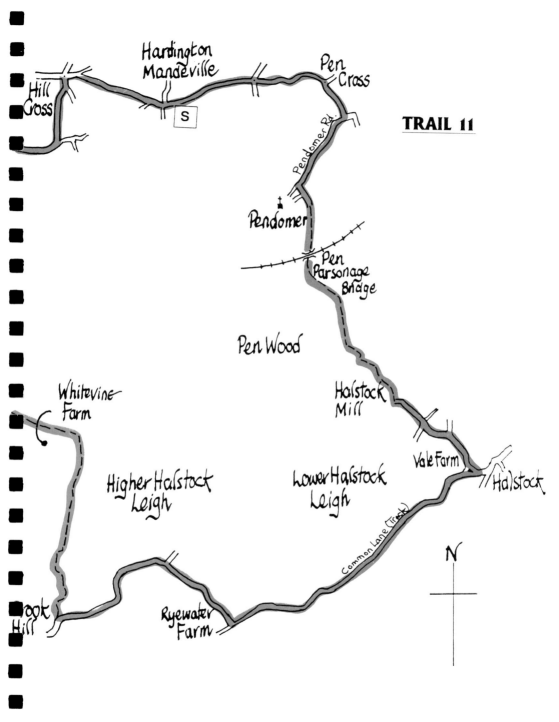

Hartington
Mandeville

Pen
Cross

Hill
Cross

S

TRAIL 11

Pendomer Rd.

Pendomer

Pen
Parsonage
Bridge

Pen Wood

Whitevine
Farm

Halstock
Mill

Vale Farm

Halstock

Higher Halstock
Leigh

Lower Halstock
Leigh

Common Lane (Track)

N

ook
Hill

Ryewater
Farm

SEABOROUGH/ CLAPTON/OATHILL/ WINSHAM

TRAIL 12

A 14 MILE CIRCULAR TRAIL (CLOCKWISE)

Ordnance Survey Maps:
Pathfinder: 1297
Landranger: 193

Parking & Starting Points:
Parking is available at Henley Cross (GR.434077) which is situated just outside Crewkerne off the Lyme Regis road. This is also your starting point.

Parking Note: Parking is also available on the lay-by in Shave Lane, the lay-by outside Higher Folly Farm (GR.432078), and by prior arrangement at Hill View Stables - Telephone (0460) 72731.

Of Interest:
This scenic route has good views through quiet unspoilt countryside. You may well see herons and buzzards on your ride. Clapton Court Gardens are one of Somerset's most beautiful, including amongst its collection of trees, plants and shrubs, the oldest and largest Ash tree in England which is over 220 years old and 28 feet in girth. The village of Winsham borders Dorset and Somerset and is known by the older folk as Winsum. It is a pretty village with 8 thatched cottages. The church dates back to the 13th Century. One villager whose family has long resided in Winsham remembers: 'Memories remain of my Grandfather Good, who in younger life, worked at the cloth factory, for which he used to collect folks' urine in the days of no flush toilets. This was used to soak cloth and the families who produced the most were given a length of cloth at Christmas, a real treat!' Crewkerne is a

most attractive historic old country market town set in the beautiful hilly South Somerset countryside about 30 minutes drive from the coast. Its origins go well back into Saxon times and in the middle ages it prospered as an agricultural and market centre. The wool boom of the late 15th Century enabled it to rebuild its church on a magnificent scale. It is one of the finest amongst the many famous medieval churches in Somerset.

Route Description:

The route starts at Henley Cross (GR.434077) which is situated just outside Crewkerne, off the Lyme Regis road. Cross straight over Henley crossroads riding in a southerly direction for 1.25 miles to descend a steep hill and pass a junction on your left. Note the beautiful views here on either side of the road. **Turn right 50 yards after the junction into a farm track to ride straight on through West Dairy Farm and out through the field gate. You are now briefly in Dorset. Ride straight on following the track until you reach two farm gates ahead of you where you go through the left gate. Follow the track with a stream on your left. The track opens out into a small field. Continue along the track to reach a small hunting gate. Go through the gate and ride diagonally to your right across the field, over the brow of a hill and down to a gate leading onto a track. Ride along this track to the farm**

and out onto a road (B3165) **TAKING GREAT CARE, where you turn left (GR.415065).**

Continue along this road. *You will pass the famous Clapton Mill which is a fine example of a working water mill.* **Having passed Clapton Mill, continue on going over the stone bridge and on up the hill. After approximately one mile, as you round a bend you will approach some isolated houses**. *On your right is Lower Oathill Farm, which is clearly signposted*

and distinguished by the large artificial spider and web in the front circular window. **Immediately past the farmhouse is a track which is the beginning of a further bridleway (GR.405057).** *It is possible to mistake this for the farm drive.*

Turn here, go through two gates and proceed along an enclosed track into a field. *You will go through some charming wooded countryside in this part of the ride.*

TRAIL 12

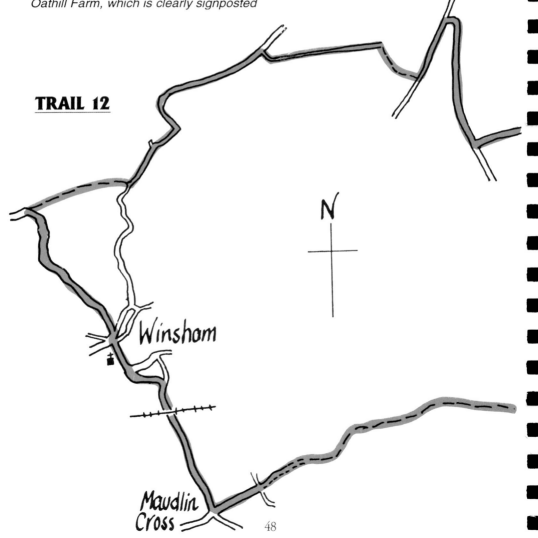

N

Winsham

Maudlin Cross

48

Head straight on from the end of the track towards the trees to come to a gate. Go through the gate, across another small field and through the next gate. You are now in a 'green lane' with the River Axe bordered by trees to your right. Follow this green lane for its length, which is about one mile. At the end it drops down towards a stream and into a field. Cross this field and go into the next field. *There may be sheep wire erected in this second field but this is set into the field to allow free passage along the bridleway which runs around the left hand field boundary and along a further track.* Continuing on, the track passes

Beer Farm House and joins their farm driveway. Follow the drive for 0.50 miles past two cattle grids - there are gates at the side of each - to join the Greenham/Winsham road at Maudlin Cross (B3162)(GR.382052). Turn right.

If you turn left here instead of right you will find The Squirrel Inn 0.25 miles along the road. It makes a good refreshment stop.

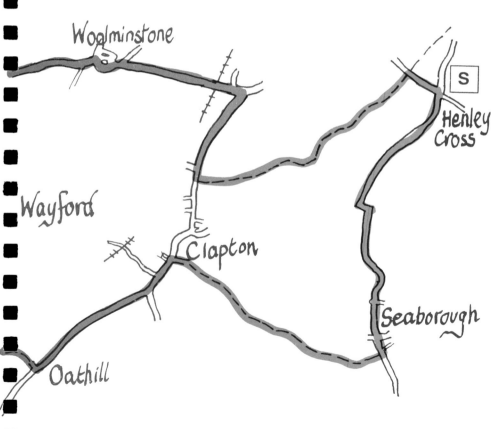

Follow the road for one mile to the village of Winsham passing The Bell Inn and continue to the Cross. Take the second turning right by the Cross - both turns are together! After a few yards turn left up Colham Lane and continue along here for 0.50 miles. This lane meanders, drops down into a valley past a house called Hollowells and then goes over a tiny hump-backed bridge. A few yards further on turn right (GR.368074) and onto a farm track called Chalkway. Follow this track until you meet a road where you turn left. Ride along this road for one mile ignoring the first bridleway sign to Lue Farm and take the bridleway to the right signposted Green Lane. Follow the enclosed track for 0.66 miles to a bridlegate. Go through the gate and turn right along the track. Before reaching the farm buildings you will come to a bridlegate leading into a field on your left. *It is not easy to spot this gate.* Go through the gate and follow the edge of the field passing the farm buildings on your right, to reach a road (GR.396083). Turn left along the road.

Follow the road and take the first right turn into Chard Lane. Take the next turn left and ride down the hill to Woolminstone. When you reach a branch in the road, take the right branch to reach the Clapton road. Turn right here and continue for 0.50 miles to turn left into Clapton Dairy Farm. Follow the track through the middle of a field to a bridlegate. Go through this bridlegate and continue along the track going through the next field and two more bridlegates. *You will see signs warning you of badger holes!* The bridleway then crosses the middle of the next field, the initial hedge to the right giving you the straight direction to follow. The field subsequently opens out and the hedge drops away.

Go through the bridlegate on the other side of the field and into the last field, keeping the hedge on your left. On reaching a road, turn right and ride on to the top of the hill and Henley Cross, your starting point.

Cottage just before the Minster Square, the market place just before

SAFETY

Know your Highway Code (1994 Edition)

In Particular Paragraphs 216/224

RIDE WITH:

CARE

- For the Land

COURTESY

- To other users

CONSIDERATION

- For the Farmer

Disclaimer

Whilst all due care was taken in the preparation of these maps neither the British Horse Society nor their agents or servants accept any responsibility for any inaccuracies which may occur. It should be borne in mind that landmarks and conditions change and it is assumed that the user has a Pathfinder or Landranger Ordnance Survey map and a compass.

The Country Code should be observed by every rider, with great care being taken to keep to the line of the Public Rights of Way particularly when crossing farmland.

THORNEY/ WEST MOOR/ MUCHELNEY

TRAIL 13

AN 11 MILE CIRCULAR TRAIL (ANTI-CLOCKWISE)

Ordnance Survey Maps:
Landranger: 193
Pathfinder: 1259 & 1279

Parking & Starting Point:
Parking is available at Thorney Lakes Campsite & Lakes (GR.429232) by prior arrangement. Please telephone: (0458) 250811.

Parking Note: At Thorney Lakes Campsite & Lakes please park just inside the gates, on the left hand side. It is necessary to telephone to confirm that there is space available.

Cautionary Note:
1.   Most of the area of West Moor used for this ride is low-lying and is therefore wet and muddy after any spell of heavy rain, and particularly during the winter. It is best enjoyed from May to October.

2.   The rhynes (drainage ditches), dividing the fields on West Moor, are deep with soft muddy bottoms. **Please be very careful along this part of the trail.**

Of Interest:
You will often see herons, swans and buzzards along the route. Sometimes mink can be seen in the rhynes and deer occasionally graze near the withy beds.

Route Description:

From your parking place at Thorney Lakes Campsite & Lakes (GR.429232),
return to the gateway and turn left onto the road and ride over the old railway bridge. Continue along the road going over the bridge across the River Parrett and so on into Thorney. Turn right, WITH CARE, across the bend at Duck's Corner and ride onto the Newmead Drove. After about 0.66 miles turn left onto Thorney Drove. When you meet the crossing of Droveways at Summerway Bridge, turn right onto Pitt Drove, crossing over Westmoor Main Drain at Pitt Bridge. *You have super views of Burrow Hill (known locally as One Tree Hill), where Burrow Hill Cider and Cider Brandy is made; Kingsbury Church tower, Montacute and Ham Hill to the south-east. To your right is the wooded hump of Midelney.**

At the T-junction of droves, turn left on to Middle Drove, cross the Main Drain again at Hurst Bridge and then after 0.66 miles turn right onto Burrow Drove. *This end can be badly rutted but improves about half-way along.* You can see the Withy beds on your right. These are Willow Trees grown for basket making.

On reaching the Hambridge to Burrow Hill road (GR.405209), turn left and on reaching Burrow Hill Farm on your left with May Farm on the right corner, go sharp right to continue along the road. Pass Higher Burrow Farm and Ocmis Irrigation and go up the hill. Ride straight past the junction, with One Tree Hill on your left and Pass Vale Farm on your right. *Pass Vale Farm is*

TRAIL 13

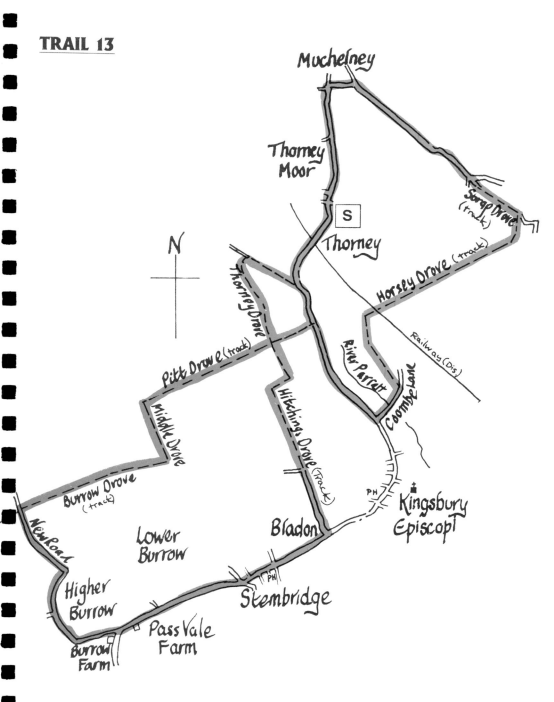

Muchelney

Thorney Moor

S

Thorney

Scrap Drove (track)

Horsey Drove (track)

Thorney Drove

Pitt Drove (track)

River Parrett

Railway (Dis)

N

Middle Drove

Coombe Lane

Hitchings Drove (track)

Burrow Drove (track)

New Road

Lower Burrow

Bladon

PH

Kingsbury Episcopi

Higher Burrow

Pass Vale Farm

Burrow Farm

PH

Stembridge

the home of Burrow Hill cider and brandy.
Continue on the road riding down the hill to come to the Rusty Axe Public House and then ride carefully along the short stretch of busier road. Turn left on to the side road at Bladon (GR.429206) and continue northwards on Hitchings Drove back to Summerway Bridge.

Turn right and ride along Pitt Drove until you meet the Kingsbury to Muchelney road where you turn right again. Ride along this road in a southerly direction, towards Kingsbury. In approximately 0.75 miles turn left into Coombe Lane. Cross the River Parrett at Coombe Bridge and then turn down the Drove which branches off to the left. Cross over the old railway line going through the two gates and onto Horsey Drove and Strap Drove. *For reasons unknown, the locals refer to this area as Egypt.*

Aim for the far corner of the last field and go through the gate and onto a road. Turn left along the road for approximately 1.25 miles to Muchelney. *To the north of you is Muchelney Church which has one of the few remaining barrel organs. There are marvellous views from the top of the tower. If you visit the annual fete on August Bank Holiday Monday you can go up the tower for a small fee, and its free to come down again! At the top you will also see the graffiti of several centuries and shoe outlines cut into the lead floor.*

In Muchelney, turn left along the street and then left again, in a southerly direction along the road back to Thorney and so to your parking place at Thorney Lakes.

ROUND COTLEY & WAMBROOK

TRAIL 14

A 13 MILE CIRCULAR TRAIL (ANTI-CLOCKWISE)

Ordnance Survey Maps:
Landranger: 193
Pathfinder: 1297

Parking & Starting Points:
Parking is available at The Poppe Inn at Tatworth or in the lay-by between Tatworth Church and the A358 (GR.326058). The route is described from here.

NOTE: Parking is also available at several points along the route, as given below. If you choose to start your ride at any of these, the ride must be picked up in the appropriate place in the text.

Parking is available:
GR.303068 - Wide grass verges along Green Lane.
GR.283058 - Wide grass verges near Broad Croft Cross.
GR.277074 - Wide grass verges near Mounter's Hill Cross.
GR.273071 - Lay-by in James Cross Lane.

Of Interest:
This ride is in an unspoilt and rural corner of Somerset and the fringes of Devon, all within the Blackdown Hills Area of Outstanding Natural Beauty. It is however, a very stony area, several of the bridleways are rough and can only be ridden at the walk. To compensate, nearly all the fields are grass, the views delightful, and the wildlife abundant.

Route Description:

Cross the main A358 Chard to Axminster road, WITH CARE, and take the bridleway running due west, leaving Parrocks Lodge on your right. Where the main track bears left, ride straight on along a narrow, enclosed bridleway to a bridlegate. Ride straight across the next open field to come to another bridlegate. Go through the gate and turn right into a narrow lane and continue along this lane to another bridlegate. Go through this gate and follow the headland along the left hand hedge to a farm gate leading out onto a road (GR.316060). *You are now in Devon.*

Go through this gate and onto a road and turn right, then at the next road junction, turn left. Follow this road round to the left and into Burridge. At the barn and cottage on the corner, bear left and continue down a small road towards Hook. Bear right round the bend and over the stream and just 15 yards before the crossroads at Hook Cross, go sharply back to the right. *This track is an unclassified county road and therefore not signposted.* Ride along this track and through the middle of Burridge Common. Keep straight on until you join a hard stony track and continue along here going left up a hill to a road.

Almost immediately turn right along Green Lane with its very wide grass

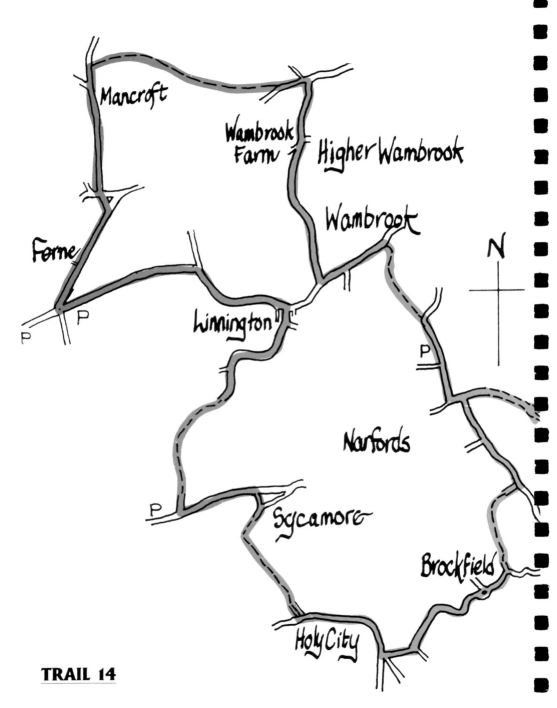

Mancroft

Wambrook
Farm

Higher Wambrook

Wambrook

Ferne

P
P
P

Limmington

N

P

Narfords

P

Sycamore

Brockfield

Holy City

TRAIL 14

verges on both sides. *You are now back in Somerset. The Cotley Point-to-Point fences can be seen in the fields on your right. Racing takes place on the first Bank Holiday Monday in May.* **Where the road turns right, ride straight on through a field gate and down the bridleway signposted to Wambrook.**

Follow the track along the left hand hedge, riding straight ahead. Go through two more gates and into a steep lane. *Go carefully here, the track is narrow and stony.* **On meeting a road turn left and follow it down past Cotley Inn.** *The Cotley Inn can provide bed and breakfast for both horse and rider, excellent meals and even has a hitching rail outside. In summer, you can eat in the garden alongside the hitching rail.*

Having passed Cotley Inn, take the first turning right (GR.294075) and ride on up through the village, passing the little 14th Century Church on your right.

On reaching a T-junction at the very top, turn left (GR.293088). Immediately on your right is the entrance to Weston Farm. Your route goes to the left of the entrance and up a bank, to continue through a bridlegate which opens into a series of grass fields. Follow the bridleway through these fields keeping the hedge to the left all the way. There are a total of six gates along this long bridleway, but with a handy horse, you should be able to manage them all without dismounting.

At the end of the bridleway you will ride along a short avenue of Beech trees and so re-join the road (GR.278090). Turn left along the road and ride due south along the top of the hill. After passing the Ferne Animal Sanctuary on your right, you will come to a crossroads known as Mounters Hill Cross (GR.276074). *There are lovely views here across the valley.*

At Mounter's Hill Cross crossroads, turn left and follow a quiet little road with a good grass verge, for just over 0.50 miles. At the first junction, bear right and continue riding downhill back

Burridge

Hook

P Tatworth

S

At the top of the village you pass Wambrook Farm on your left. Bed and breakfast for horse and rider is available here and there is ample parking.

towards Wambrook village until you come to the next sharp turn to your right, marked 'No Through Road'. Ride down this 'No Through Road' which leads into a bridleway through the woods, which are full of rhododendrons in early summer. *You are now back in Devon.*

57

The end of this bridleway will bring you back to a road where you turn left (GR.284059) and ride downhill and take the next turning right. This bridleway runs round behind some cottages, through a wood and out across a big grass field to Woonton Farm. The trail runs to the west of the farm buildings, through a gate and down the farm drive. At the end of the farm drive, when you meet a road, turn left along the road.

Ride along the road to the next crossroads, passing the few houses which make up the quaintly named Holy City, and turn left (GR.298049). Ride by a scatter of houses called Farway, through the dip and then, where the lane is very narrow, ride through the ford and on up towards Hook.

At the T-junction at Brockfield (GR.306055), where the road goes right to Hook, turn left between the two cottages and take the bridleway. This bridleway is steep and stony at first, but soon becomes a nice, green lane. On reaching the end of the bridleway you will meet the road. Turn left and ride up Huntley Lane. At the T-junction at the top of the lane, turn right and ride back across Burridge Common, but this time ride along the hard stony track which runs round the top of the Common to Burridge. On leaving the Common, retrace your steps to Tatworth and your parking place.

Wambrook Stocks

Grain Store

THE QUANTOCKS

TRAIL 15

A 18 MILE CIRCULAR TRAIL (ANTI-CLOCKWISE)

Ordnance Survey Maps:
Landranger: 181
Pathfinder: 1216

Parking & Starting Point:
Parking is available in the designated parking area amongst the trees at Ramscombe (GR.165377). This is also your starting point.

Parking Note: Ramscombe is best approached from the A39 via Nether Stowey or Over Stowey and Adscombe where you take the Quantock Forest Trail sign to the parking areas in the trees where there is a pleasant stream to water horses. There are also public toilets available here.

Of Interest:
This ride has very wide, interesting tracks, with every sort of scenery, all glorious. Open moors, woodland, deer and pony grazing country, sheltered valleys and ancient tree-lined tracks. A lovely area to ride without the dangers of bog, cliff edges, or the worry of being lost forever. It is quite possible to be on a track which was not intended as there are so many converging, and no signs to show if they are deer tracks, bridleways, forestry tracks, fire breaks etc. but the area is so soft, friendly, cosy, varied and lovely that it does not really matter; it is impossible to get lost, in fact all roads lead to home!

The Quantock Wardens are extremely helpful and can be telephoned at the Nether Stowey Wardens Office (0278) 732845 if *you require information of any kind. The Wardens have also kindly waymarked this route for riders and other users. The waymark is a special Quantock Ride sign, being the same style as the circular walk sign but with a **blue** circle and a white arrow on a black background. The general policy is for no signs at all on the Quantocks to keep the area as wild as possible, which is great, but of course impossible to describe any route for riders to follow. The Pathfinder map 1216 is strongly recommended, as it contains the whole of the Quantocks on one sheet.*

Route Description:

From the parking area, follow the one-way system through the wood and back towards Adscombe. Just before you reach the cattle grid you crossed to come into the parking area, turn sharp left (GR.179378) to take the forest track through Seven Wells Wood. Continue straight on along the track towards Great Bear to come to the metalled road (GR.169383). *This road runs from Bincombe Green in the east to Crowcombe Park Gate in the west.* **Turn left and take the track parallel with the road and ride along as far as the Dead Womans Ditch parking area. Take the bridleway opposite and slightly to your left riding south of Robin Upnights Hill and continue straight on across the first bridleways crossroads to turn right at the second crossroads of bridleways (GR.148384). Continue across the top of the open moor - Higher Hare Knapp**

TRAIL 15

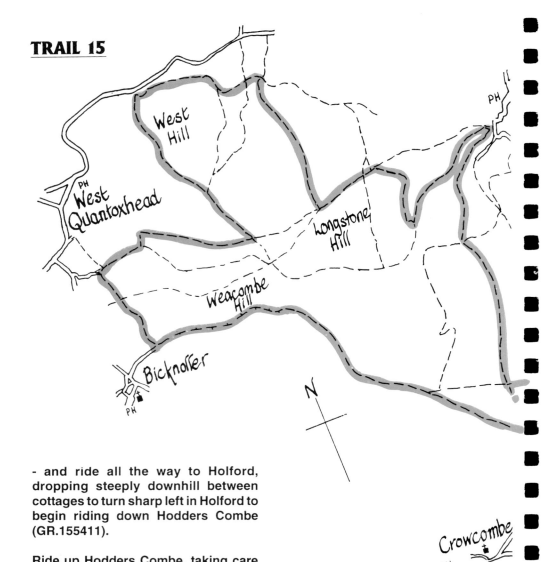

- and ride all the way to Holford, dropping steeply downhill between cottages to turn sharp left in Holford to begin riding down Hodders Combe (GR.155411).

Ride up Hodders Combe, taking care not to miss the bridleway to your right where you turn to cross the watercourse, going up through the trees to bear right up to Willoughby Cleeve then left crossing the open moor (Longstone Hill) to New Ground to meet a RUPP (GR.142410). Turn left along the RUPP and ride on the open moor. *There are wonderful views all around and on a windy day it can be really blustery here.*

Take the next bridleway to your right to ride across more open moor (East Quantoxhead) to Higher Ground (GR.134423), then turn left taking the bridleway running east to west, south of the A39 around the side of the hill to Perry and Perry Combe Plantation (GR.121425). *This bridleway has a high deer-wire fence running along all the way on your right-hand side. There are*

60

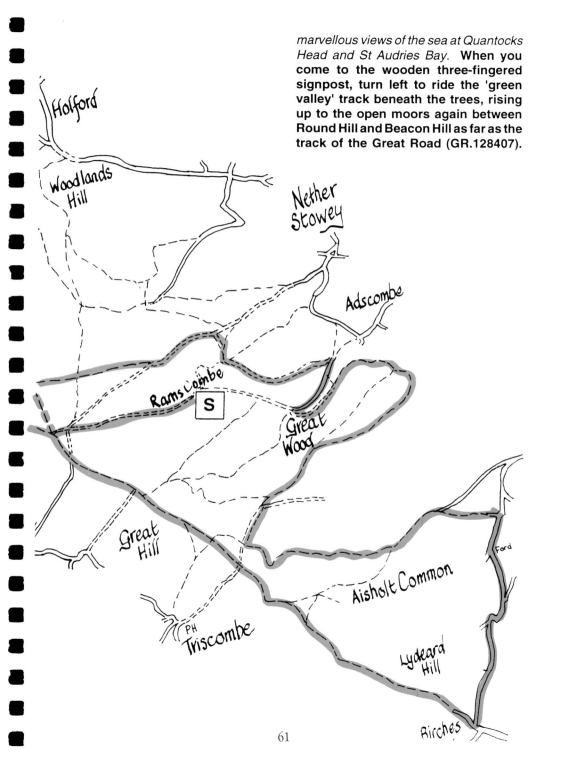

marvellous views of the sea at Quantocks Head and St Audries Bay. **When you come to the wooden three-fingered signpost, turn left to ride the 'green valley' track beneath the trees, rising up to the open moors again between Round Hill and Beacon Hill as far as the track of the Great Road (GR.128407).**

Turn right and ride west on the Great Road across Beacon Hill and take the next turn left on the edge of the wood, then the bridleway to the right to Weacombe. Follow round on the west of Round Plantation and ride straight across at the next bridleway crossing to continue south by Haslett Plantation. Cross over the next junction of tracks to a RUPP (Bicknoller Combe) (GR.115398). Turn left along a RUPP riding east on Bicknoller Combe (Bicknoller Hill) and ride straight over the next bridleway crossing staying on the main track all the way to Crowcombe Park Gate (GR.149378) on the ridge of Thorncombe Hill by Halsway Soggs and Hurley Beacon.

At this point if you wish to shorten your ride, it is possible to take the track to the left and go back to Ramscombe, staying south of the disused quarry through the woods.

To complete the main ride: Continue straight on down the main track, crossing the metalled road at Crowcombe Combe Gate and ride along this very wide RUPP. *This is tree-lined with lovely views on either side. The views are even better when the leaves have left the trees.* Stay on this RUPP around the corner of The Slades Wood and take the right branch RUPP at Black Knap (GR.167354). Continue south on this RUPP riding south of Middle Hill and north-east of Bagborough Plantation, and so continue on south of Lydeard Hill to the car park at the north-west corner of Muchcare Wood. *Here there is a short distance of steepish, sunken, narrow metalled road but it is possible to ride through the wood just above and to the side of the road - this a permissive route granted by the farmer to make for safer riding.*

Turn sharp left at the southern edge of the wood at Birches Corner (GR.183335). Follow this track north along the side of Muchcare Wood, stay right at the top of the wood and then in a short distance take the next left turn and continue travelling north on the track to the east of Durborough Farm. Ride through the ford as far as Higher Aisholt Farm. *The very pretty village of Aisholt is to the east where there is only a small church and a few picturesque cottages.* Turn left above Higher Aisholt Farm and ride along the bridleway to the southern edge of Parsons Plantation (GR.185359).

Turn left and ride along with the wood on your right and glorious views to your left. After about 800 yards go through a hunting gate on the right and take the track to the left which runs diagonally through The Slades. Ignore the turning where the track turns sharp right to go back along Cockercombe Bottom and ride straight on as far as the metalled road (GR.165361). Turn right along the side of this stretch of road and ride for a short distance, then as the road bends right, go straight on through the gate beside a cattle grid and so into Great Wood. Stay on this semi-metalled, wide track, between Hart Hill and Dibble's Firs. *There are lovely views here.* Stay north of Floorey Down, riding along Keepers Combe.

Take the left-hand bridlepath around the edge of the wood, up a grassy track to a junction. Turn left here, staying west of the school and round the north-east edge of Great Wood. Stay on the bridleway heading for Great Wood Campsite and so return to the Ramscombe Parking Area by riding down the hill on a very wide track.

THE BRITISH HORSE SOCIETY

The British Horse Society was founded in 1947 when two separate equestrian bodies - The National Horse Association and the Institute of the Horse and Pony Club - decided to join forces and work together for the good of both horse and rider.

It is a marriage that has proved to be a great success and the British Horse Society has steadily increased its membership from just 4000 in the late 1960's to over 60,000 in the 1990's.

By becoming members of the British Horse Society, horse lovers know they are joining a body of people with a shared interest in the horse. Members can be sure that they are contributing to the work of an equine charity with a primary aim to improve the standards of care for horses and ponies. Welfare is not only about the rescuing of horses in distress (which we do); it is also about acting to prevent abuse in the first place. There are many means to achieving this: by teaching and advising, by looking to the horse's well-being and safety, by providing off-road riding, by encouraging high standards in all equestrian establishments, and fighting for the horse's case with government and in Europe.

The British Horse Society works tirelessly towards these aims thanks to the work of its officials at Stoneleigh and its army of dedicated volunteers out in the field.

Membership benefits the horse lover as well as the horse; the Society can offer something to all equestrians, whether they are weekend riders, interested spectators or keen competitors. The benefits include free Third Party Public Liability and Personal Accident insurance, free legal advice, free publications, reductions to British Horse Society events, special facilities at the major shows, and free advice and information on any equine query.

Largely financed by its membership subscriptions, the Society welcomes the support of all horse lovers. If you are thinking of joining the Society and would like to find out more about our work, please contact the Membership Department at the following address:

The British Horse Society
British Equestrian Centre
Stoneleigh Park
Kenilworth
Warwickshire
CV8 2LR
(Telephone: 0203 696697)
Registered Charity No. 210504